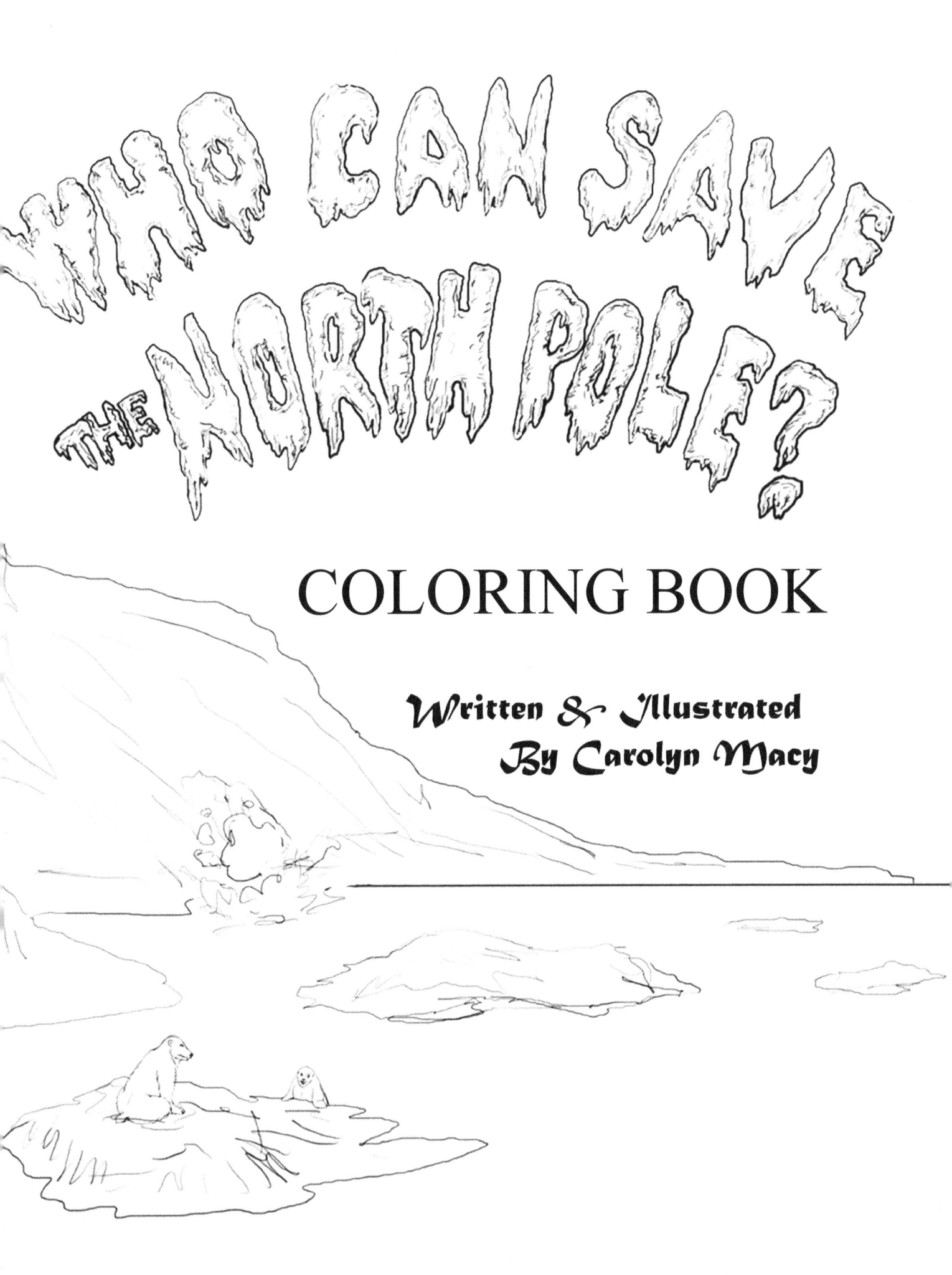

Dedicated to my family and friends.

Who Can Save the North Pole Coloring Book
Copyright © 2017 by Carolyn Macy. All rights reserved.

No part of this publication may be reproduced, stored in a retrieval system or transmitted in any way by any means, electronic, mechanical, photocopy, recording or otherwise without the prior permission of the author except as provided by USA copyright law.

Published by Carolyn Macy
6227 81st Avenue N.E. | Norman, Oklahoma 73026 USA
405.401.2012

Book design copyright © 2017 by Carolyn Macy.
Written and Illustrated by Carolyn Macy

Published in the United States of America
ISBN: 978-0-9989127-9-0
1. JUVENILE FICTION / General
2. SCIENCE / Earth Science / Meteorology & Climatology

The sun was still shining
   And lit up the night
On the sea to the North
   That was frozen and white.

It hung very low,
   Still ablaze in the sky,
And lighted the icecap
   Where reindeer can fly.

Sharp sounds in the ice
   Caused the reindeer to pause,
Then fly to the workshop
   To tell Santa Claus.

So off they all went
   To see what they could see,
And to search for the sounds
   And what caused them to be.

They followed those sounds and to much their surprise
　　The icecap was changing in front of their eyes!
Its cliffs of ice rumbled as chunks crashed below,
　　With reservoirs formed from a meltwater flow.

The animals caught in this arctic upset
　　Were seeking for safety away from its threat.
So troubling were things that were seen on this trek.
　　That Santa dashed home to review and reflect.

What brought all the changes disrupting the ice?
   From what he had seen, Santa searched for advice.
He talked to the people who studied the ocean
   And learned of some things that could cause this commotion

With red diving gear, Santa dove in the sea
   To search for what mischief had caused this to be.
From its sheets of thin ice to its murky, deep floor,
   Santa found that pollutants and heat measured more

He sent a balloon to zoom
   High in the air
To check what had happened
   With things found up there.

Facts learned from the experts
   On things about weather,
Showed air and the ocean
   And land worked together.

Some fumes put in air that were raising concern,
  Come from fuels that our cars and the factories burn.
Instead of returning the hot solar glare,
  Those gases then held its hot heat in the air.

Soon oceans grow warmer as temperatures climb,
  And polar ice melts from this warmth over time.
Less ice to reflect the sun's light rays and heat,
  Adds warming for melting the polar ice sheet.

Our oceans and trees help
Control these conditions
By clearing the air
Of some carbon emissions.

The trees give off oxygen into the air,
  Using carbon dioxide for growth and repair.
 When an excess of cutting gets rid of the trees,
  Then soil is left bare to be swept off with ease.

Our use of the water to dump many things
   Makes more harmful damage than answers it brings.
As wastes are received from the land and the air,
   Then oceans are changed for the life living there.

Recycling of trash that's no longer in use
   Helps clean up some clutter from what we produce.

After looking for answers to changes he saw,
   Santa thought about causes that brought on the thaw.
This gained understanding of facts he now knew,
   Helped Santa decide on just what he should do.

He made some arrangements for charting his way,
   And clearing the flights he would take in his sleigh.
To ask for their help in these problems for all,
   Santa placed to the newsmen an urgent phone call.

After sharing his plans about where they could meet,
   He whistled and called for his four-footed fleet.

His team was all hitched and was ready to go
   When again they heard rumblings rise up from below.
"On Mystique and Melton and Leaper and Lazer!
   Fly Beacon and Boomer and Mischief and Blazer!"

Away they all flew in a speedy commute,
   Wearing oxygen masks along parts of their route.
Though coughing and wheezing, the team made it through,
   And felt lucky to land near a main avenue.

A crowd had assembled as Santa flew in
   And landed his sleigh in their midst with a grin.
He stepped from the sleigh, gazing quickly at each,
   Then cleared his throat softly and started his speech.

He spoke of the rumblings heard day after day,
  As ice on the icecap kept melting away.
Santa told of the problems he faced at North Pole,
  And how using things wisely would lessen their toll.

The sun shines upon us day in and day out,
 And makes the wind move all around and about.
Available always for use and control,
 They help to create a clean energy role."

"Our tots, you're our future and now just for you
 We must make needed changes and follow them through!
Though it's hard to find answers that help solve our plight.
 We know what is wrong, and we must make it right!"

"By the time of my visit on Christmas Eve night,
Let's do what we can to start setting things right."

www.ingramcontent.com/pod-product-compliance
Lightning Source LLC
Chambersburg PA
CBHW080416300426
44113CB00015B/2542